This Notebook Belongs to :

Printed in Great Britain
by Amazon

77523010R00072